SONGS and STORIES T

Music Activities for the
Early Childhood Classroom

SALLY GUERRERO

Alfred Music
16320 Roscoe Blvd., Suite 100
P.O. Box 10003
Van Nuys, CA 91410-0003

Alfred

alfred.com

Copyright © 2012 by Alfred Music
All Rights Reserved.   Printed In USA.
ISBN-10: 0-7390-8839-4
ISBN-13: 978-0-7390-8839-5

Table of Contents

> *I dedicate this book to my two boys, Mark and Michael, who, in their early childhood years,*
> *ignited the desire within me to follow the path of early childhood music education.*

Acknowledgments

To all the children (and their parents) of the Pasadena Conservatory of Music, where I taught for almost twenty years, who listened to the stories, heard the beautiful classical music, sang the songs and played the games; it was in your eyes that I saw the reflection of love that beautiful art can bring to people of all ages.

Thank you to my friends who encouraged me to write this book and not give up on the idea: to Cecilia Riddell for suggesting I do this in the first place; to Stephen McCurry who has always loved the story and classical music connection; to my dearest friends Barbara Patton Unger and Camille Hayes; to Richard Brazill and to my many esteemed colleagues.

Preface

This unique book for early childhood educators connects songs to stories and classical music with activities that build music skills through singing, moving, listening and playing classroom instruments. I have used these songs, stories and activities in my classroom and know that they are fun and engaging. In general, the activities are appropriate for children ages 3–6 years. You can determine the developmental appropriateness of each activity based on your individual classroom situation and children's abilities. Teachers who have a modest music background can teach most of the activities. However, the ensemble activities, last in each sequence, are designed to be taught by teachers who do have a music background and can be used in developing ensemble skills in children at least 6 years of age.

When I first began teaching, I loved introducing children to classical music and increasing their ability to enjoy and own this music. My mission as an early childhood music educator developed out of this love. The activities in this book accomplish important goals: to teach singing and steady beat while engaging children's minds, bodies, and imaginations; to expand children's appreciation of good quality music and literature.

A quote by Hungarian composer and music educator, Zoltàn Kodàly, has inspired my work with young children: "Real art is one of the most powerful forces in the rise of [humankind], and [she or he] who renders it accessible to as many people as possible is a benefactor of humanity."

And I love what Albert Einstein said about music and imagination, "Imagination is more important than knowledge." "If I were not a physicist, I would probably be a musician. I often think in music. I live my daydreams in music. I see my life in terms of music. I get most joy in life out of music."

It is a privilege and opportunity to work with very young children. Why not bring them in contact with "real art" and inspire them to be imaginative through the beauty of music? As early childhood educators, I hope you find the songs, stories, and classical music suggested in this book to be a powerful force for good in the lives of many children and that the music will inspire the most creative and positive aspects of their imaginations.

How to Use This Book

In general, this book is organized alphabetically by song titles. For each song, there are activities for teaching the song, a story, and classical music relating to the story. There are further activities that provide opportunities to develop the song and to reinforce listening to classical music through movement and instrument play. As you read through the activities, you can decide what you feel comfortable teaching and what is appropriate for the age and developmental abilities of your students. For example, some of the stories are more appropriate for pre-school children, but I have used them with first grade children depending on the goals I wish to accomplish.

You will notice I use some musical terms which are familiar to music educators such as the solfège language of Sol and Mi, ensemble, ostinato, pentatonic, and others. If you are not familiar with some of the terms or how to implement a concept, you can skip those activities. The ensemble activities will be most useful for music educators who have experience using xylophones and other barred instruments. Most of the songs are written in the key of C or D major but music educators can transpose them to suit your needs.

You will find the activities useful in addressing many skills besides musical skills: visual, spatial, aural, verbal, kinesthetic, interpersonal, and intrapersonal skills.

Here is what you will need to use this book:
1. Storybooks (see Bibliography/Discography), all of which are in print and can be found in bookstores or websites. You'll find many in your school library, and used books are another excellent source.

2. Recordings of classical music (see Bibliography/Discography). Each can be purchased for $0.99 on iTunes. I have been very specific as to which recordings go best with each story and have given details, such as the name of the album and artist so you can find the exact recording on iTunes. Once you have collected all the musical selections, you will be able to play them frequently, using different activities from this book.

3. Percussion instruments such as finger cymbals, triangles, sticks, resonator bells, xylophones, metallophones, and glockenspiels. You can mix and match and use the instruments you currently have.

4. Scarves and a few other props, which are easily made or acquired.

The songs, stories, and recordings are classic. Children love hearing them over and over. As you and the children become familiar with them, their love for the music and literature will grow. It is my hope that this book will serve you for many, many years.

All 'Round the Barnyard

Folk Song
Adapted by Sally Guerrero

All 'round the barn-yard re - mem - ber me, I'm gon - na

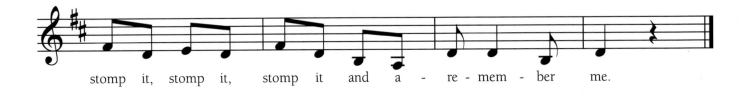

stomp it, stomp it, stomp it and a - re - mem - ber me.

Additional verses: (*cumulatively add actions here*)

All 'round the barn-yard re - mem - ber me, I'm gon - na clap it, clap it,

clap it, stomp it, stomp it, stomp it and a - re - mem - ber me.

Storybook: *Barnyard Dance*
Recording: "The Happy Farmer" by Robert Schumann

Hint: The goal is for children to sing the song independently before adding movement or instruments. To accomplish this, I teach the song using hand motions to replicate the movement that will come later.

Activity 1: Introduce the song "All 'Round the Barnyard."
- Sing the first part of the song, "All 'round the barnyard, remember me we're gonna," using alternating hand patting.
- To the next words, "stomp, it stomp it, stomp it," pound fists together three times.
- To the next words, "and-a remember me," make a circle in the air with your finger.
- Engage the children in creating new action words such as "jump it, jump it, jump it" or "clap it, clap it, clap it" using hand motions to represent the action words.
- Add the new words and actions in a cumulative fashion. As you do this and recall the sequence, you are helping build memory skills.

Activity 2: All stand in a circle and play a movement game.
- Hold hands. Circle to the right while singing "All 'round the barnyard, remember me we're gonna."
- Stop and perform each action while singing "stomp it, stomp it, stomp it," etc.
- Turn in place while singing "and a-remember me."
- Add new actions in a cumulative fashion.

Activity 3: Read the story *Barnyard Dance* with your preschool children as the recording of "The Happy Farmer" is playing in the background.
- Play the recording two times to complete reading the story.
- Teach musical vocabulary to describe this music: lively, happy.
- Ask what instrument is playing: piano.
- Contrast with "Petite Ouverture a Danser" (see the story *Yellow Umbrella*, p. 24).

Activity 4: Play a movement game with instruments.
- Choose two or three contrasting movement ideas from the storybook such as twirl, strut, or skitter.
- Bring out several percussion instruments.
- Ask the children to choose an instrument sound to represent each of these movements.
- All stand.
- The children listen as you play the sound and they twirl, strut, or skitter depending on the instrument they hear you play. Encourage the children to be imaginative in their interpretations of their movements.
- In another lesson, choose other movement ideas from the story and a percussion instrument to represent each.
- This is a good activity for reinforcing auditory discrimination, motor control, and for teaching movement vocabulary.

Activity 5: Design movement pictures.
- On separate sheets of paper, have the children help you design abstract pictures to represent movements such as twirl, strut, and skitter. Twirl could be a spiral; strut could be a series of short, straight lines; skitter could be wavy lines. Be as imaginative with the representations as you like.
- All stand.
- As the music of "The Happy Farmer" is playing, hold up one picture at a time.
- Children look for the visual cues and move in ways that match the visual representation.
- In another lesson, the children create their own movement pictures and decide how they will move to them.
- This is a good activity for reinforcing visual skills.

Activity 6: Ensemble.
- First grade children can accompany their singing and moving with instruments.
- Let the students determine the sequence of movements they would like to incorporate and let them choose a percussion instrument to represent each movement.
- Sing the song and perform the movements as described in Activity 2.
- A steady beat can be played on D and A xylophone bars throughout the song; the percussion instruments are played on each action word.

All the Little Ducklings

German Folk Melody

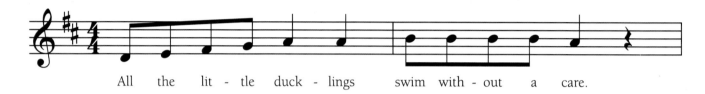

All the lit - tle duck - lings swim with - out a care.

Heads are un - der wa - ter, tails are in the air.

Storybook: *The Ugly Duckling*

Recording: "The Swan" from *Carnival of the Animals* by Camille Saint Saëns

Activity 1: Introduce the song "All the Little Ducklings."
- Sing while patting the steady beat on your knees and clapping on the rests (after the words "care" and "air").
- Transfer the claps to finger cymbals. Give children turns playing this part.

Activity 2: Play a game.
- Everyone sits in a circle on the floor.
- Choose one child to be the leader.
- The children sing, pat the beat and clap on the rests (see Activity 1) as the leader walks around the outside of the circle and taps one child on each rest.
- These children stand and follow the leader around the outside of the circle.

- The leader continues to tap one child on each rest until all children are walking behind him/her in the circle.
- With very young children, you can be the leader first as you demonstrate how the game will go. Keep in mind that the young children will not be precise in their tapping.

Activity 3: Read the story *The Ugly Duckling* as the recording of "The Swan" is playing in the background. (It usually takes one repetition of the music to finish the story.)
- Teach musical vocabulary to describe this music: smooth, sustained, slow, gentle.
- Ask what instruments are playing: piano, cello.
- Contrast with "Jazz Pizzicato" (see the story *Jump, Frog, Jump,* p. 12).

Activity 4: Unstructured movement: give each child a scarf.
- As the recording of "The Swan" is playing, encourage smooth and gentle movements.
- Children create their own movement ideas.

Activity 5: Mirror motions—structured movement.
- As the recording of "The Swan" is playing, the children stand facing you and follow as you lead slow and sustained movements with your arms and body.
- Extend this activity for first grade children. Have them choose a partner and stand facing each other.
- One partner begins leading the mirror motions as the other follows.
- You play a finger cymbal as the signal for the other partner to take over.
- This activity is good for spatial, kinesthetic, and visual learning.

Activity 6: Ensemble.
- Review the song "All the Little Ducklings" using the body percussion described in Activity 1.
- Accompany the singing while steady beat is played on D and A xylophone bars (click mallets together on rests); finger cymbals play on rests.

Activity 7: Extension.
- Music educators: here is a challenge for children who are ready.
- Practice singing the words "tails are in the air" while showing the melodic direction from high to low and keeping the clap on the rest.
- Transfer this melody to a glockenspiel and add it as an ostinato throughout the song, clicking the mallets together on the rest.
- Put this together with the ensemble parts described in Activity 6.

Buzz, Buzz, Buzz

German Folk Melody

Buzz, buzz, buzz. Bu - sy bum-ble bee. I can tell when you are com-ing

by your bu - sy buzz, buzz, buzz-ing. Buzz, buzz, buzz, bu - sy bum-ble bee.

Storybook: *Buzz, Buzz, Busy Bees*
Recording: "Flight of the Bumblebee"
by Rimsky-Korsakov

Activity 1: Sing with a puppet.
- To introduce the song "Buzz, Buzz, Buzz" you will need a bee puppet. You can make a simple finger puppet with two yellow pompoms and a black pipe cleaner. Glue the two pompoms together and wrap the black pipe cleaner around them making a loop that looks like wings and for your finger to go through.
- Tell the children that the puppet will come out on the words "buzz, buzz, buzz" (two times in the song).
- Sing the song showing the puppet on the words "buzz, buzz, buzz" and hiding the puppet when you sing the other words.
- After a few repetitions, ask the children to learn to sing the "buzz, buzz, buzz" words while you sing the other words.
- Cue them on their part by bringing out the puppet when it is their turn to sing.

Activity 2: Encourage solo singing.
- When the children are comfortable singing the "buzz, buzz, buzz" words, encourage solo singing.
- Give one child the puppet and she or he sings the solos while the rest of the class sings the other words.

Activity 3: Play a guessing game while sitting in a circle.
- One child leaves the circle and hides his/her eyes.
- Choose another child to be the soloist (singing "buzz, buzz, buzz") while the rest of the class sings the other words.
- When the song is finished, the child who was hiding guesses who was singing the solo.

Activity 4: You can read the story *Buzz, Buzz, Busy Bees* to your preschool children as the recording of "Flight of the Bumblebee" is playing in the background.
- Teach musical vocabulary to describe this music: fast, tempo.
- Listen for the string instruments.
- Contrast with "Autumn" (see the story *Busy Little Squirrel*, p. 16).

Activity 5: Unstructured movement.
- Preschool children enjoy an unstructured movement activity as the recording is playing.
- Give each child a scarf and have everyone move to the music. Tell them to be ready to stop and freeze if the music stops. You control this by stopping and starting the recording.

Activity 6: Play a movement game.
- This is an activity for older children that I learned from two sources, John Feierabend and Sophia Lopez Ibor.
- All stand stationary in a circle.
- Choose one child to be "It."
- While "It" is not looking, choose another child to be the leader of the circle.
- As the recording is playing, the leader of the circle makes movement motions (hand clapping, waving, foot stomping) for all to follow.
- "It" has to guess which child is leading the motions.

Busy Little Bumble Bee

Sally Guerrero

Bu - sy lit - tle bum - ble bee, where will you land on me?

Bu - sy lit - tle bum - ble bee, land - ing on my knee.

Activity 1: Play a memory game.
- Before singing the song, decide where the "bumble-bee" will land, such as on your knee.
- Use your hands to represent the bee.
- Sing "Busy Little Bumblebee" while tapping the steady beat on your knees.
- Ask the children what other places the bee might land (nose, head) and tap the beat in these places while singing those words.
- If you want to stretch your memory skills, you can add the places where the bee lands in a cumulative fashion, singing just those words at the end of the song ("landing on my knee and landing on my nose, and landing on my head," etc.) while showing the beat in those places.

Activity 2: Play a singing game.
- When the children know the song well, play a solo singing game using the bumblebee finger puppet (see Activity 1 from the song "Buzz, Buzz, Buzz" for instructions to make the puppet).
- Let one child hold the bumblebee puppet and suggest where to tap it.
- Everyone sings the first four measures of the song while tapping the beat in that place and the child holding the bumblebee sings the last four measures as a solo.

Cloudy Weather

Traditional

Cloud - y weath - er, wind - y weath - er,

when the wind blows we all come to - geth - er.

Storybook: *Little Cloud*

Recording: No. 2 from "Four Norwegian Dances" by Edvard Grieg

Thanks to Miriam DeLap for granting me permission to use her idea to connect the story and music of *Cloudy Weather*.

Hint: The goal is for children to be able to sing the song independently before adding movement. Teach the song first while seated and keeping the steady beat on your knees.

Activity 1: Introduce the song "Cloudy Weather."
- Teach the song while sitting down and patting the steady beat on your knees.
- Pause on the word "we" (raise hands slowly while singing "we," then continue patting and singing).
- Pause for different lengths of time with each repetition of the song.
- Tell the children they must watch your hands for the cue or signal (as you raise your hands while singing the word "we") before they continue singing.
- This encourages the children to pay attention.
- Discuss other kinds of weather (chilly, rainy, etc.) and use those lyrics in the song.

Activity 2: Play a circle game.
- All stand and hold hands.
- Sing the song while walking to the right.
- Pause on the word "we" and face the center of the circle.
- On the words "all come together" everyone takes four steps (one step for each beat) into the middle of the circle.
- Then, take a big breath and make a blowing sound as everyone scoots back out.
- Repeat the game and sing about other kinds of weather.

Activity 3: Read the story *Little Cloud* as the recording of the "Norwegian Dance" is playing in the background.
- Practice timing the music so that you are reading about the airplane and the shark when you reach the fast middle section of the music, and the trees when the slow section returns.
- Teach musical vocabulary to describe this music: slow, fast, tempo.

Activity 4: Play a rhythm game.
- Purchase paper plates, big and little ones.
- The words "big" and "lit-tle" will become spoken patterns using the rhythm of the language.
- Music educators will understand that this language imitates the rhythmic value of quarter and eighth notes.
- Place a combination of four plates on the floor in front of you where the children can see.
- Recite the pattern so that the children are tracking from their left to right as they observe the plate pattern.
- A pattern could read "big, big, lit-tle, big" and so forth.
- Let the children create and read patterns using four plates.

Activity 5: Creative movement: play a shape game.
- Give each child two plates to use as props in creating his/her shape.
- Encourage shapes where the children touch one plate to the floor and one to a body part, etc.
- As the recording of "Norwegian Dance" is playing, the children move with their plates until you play a finger cymbal. This is the cue (signal) for everyone to freeze into a shape and hold it until you play the finger cymbals again.
- Play the finger cymbals several times during the slow sections.

Firefly, Firefly

Folk Song

Fire - fly, fire - fly in the night.

With a yel - low, with a yel - low, with a yel - low light.

How I like to watch you shine to - night.

Storybook: *The Very Lonely Firefly*
Recording: "Forgotten Dreams" by Leroy Anderson

Activity 1: Introduce the song "Firefly, Firefly."
- Sit in a circle and sing the song while patting the steady beat on your knees and clapping on the rests (after "night," "light," "tonight").
- Transfer the claps to finger cymbals.
- Give children turns playing this part.

Activity 2: Read the story *The Very Lonely Firefly* as the recording of "Forgotten Dreams" is playing in the background.
- Teach musical vocabulary to describe this music: gentle, peaceful, smooth.
- Ask what instruments they hear: piano (at beginning and end) and orchestra.
- Contrast with *Concerto Grosso* (see the story *Ten Little Ladybugs*, p.22).

Activity 3: Mirror motions.
- As the recording of "Forgotten Dreams" is playing, the children sit or stand facing you.
- Tell them your hand/arm movements represent the flight of the firefly.
- Moving slowly, use one hand/arm at a time and trace a pattern in the air for children to mirror.
- Stop occasionally as you place your hand on your head, shoulders, floor, etc.
- Switch to using your other hand/arm.
- Music educators, you can show the phrasing of the music by placing your hand on your head, shoulders, or floor at the end of each phrase.
- This activity reinforces visual and spatial awareness.

Activity 4: Ensemble.
- Review the song "Firefly, Firefly" using the body percussion described in Activity 1.
- Then, accompany singing with the following instruments: steady beat is played on D and A xylophone bars (click mallets together on rests); finger cymbals play on rests.
- Music educators, you can design an activity with the A section being the instruments mentioned above to accompany the singing and a B section as a solo, improvised section.
- The B section can be played on a metallophone or glockenspiel set in D pentatonic.
- A child improvises by playing any bars she or he wants to musically represent the flight or dance of the firefly.

Frog's in the Meadow

Children's Song

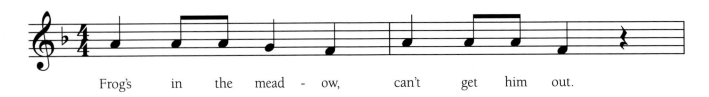

Frog's   in   the   mead - ow,   can't   get   him   out.

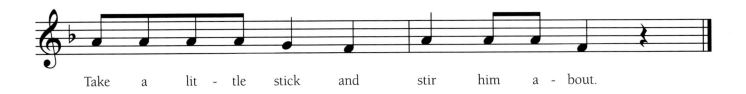

Take   a   lit - tle   stick   and   stir   him   a - bout.

Storybook: *Jump, Frog, Jump*
Recording: "Jazz Pizzicato" by Leroy Anderson

Activity 1: Introduce the song "Frog's In the Meadow."
- Make stirring motions using a different body part each time you sing (stir with finger, arm, leg, etc.).
- Ask individual children for other ways to use their body for stirring motions. Everyone follows.
- Notice if the child is moving faster or slower and sing according to the tempo (speed) she or he is using.

Activity 2: Play a guessing game.
- You will need a small plastic frog (or a cut-out of a frog, see p. 31) and four plastic cups.
- Place the four cups in a row on the floor in front of you.
- Ask the children to hide their eyes as you place the frog under one of the cups.
- Children open their eyes and sing the song "Frog's In the Meadow" as you tap the steady beat on the cups, moving from cup 1 to cup 4, and repeating this pattern until the end of the song.

- Make sure you are tapping the cups from the children's left to right and that you observe each beat of rest in the song (after the words "out" and "about").
- This is a nice visual demonstration of the four beats in each measure of the song.
- At the end, the children guess if the frog is under cup 1, 2, 3, or 4.

Activity 3: Read the story *Jump, Frog, Jump*.
- Wait to start the recording of "Jazz Pizzicato" until after you have read the first four pages.
- Ask the children to join you in speaking each time you read the words "jump, frog, jump." Teach musical vocabulary to describe the music: bouncy, jumpy, short, detached.
- Contrast with "The Swan" (see the story *The Ugly Duckling*, p. 6).

Activity 4: Play a rhythm game.

- You will need green plastic cups (to represent lily pads), and you will need cutouts of frogs and ducklings (see p. 31).
- Prepare by setting the cups upside down on the floor around the room, enough so that each child will have one.
- Place one frog or one duckling under each cup.
- Sing "Frog's In the Meadow" inserting a child's name, "...Jenny take a stick and stir him about."
- The child whose name is sung will get one cup and the frog or duckling that is underneath and bring it back to you.
- Continue until you have four.
- Set the four cups upside down in front of you and place the frog or duckling on top of each cup so the class can see.
- The frogs and ducklings become spoken rhythm patterns using the rhythm of the language.

- Recite the pattern so that the children are tracking from their left to right as they observe the pattern. A pattern might read "duck-ling, frog, duck-ling, frog" and so forth.
- Repeat the activity with a new set of four cups and frogs and ducklings.
- As in the activity for "Cloudy Weather," music educators will understand that the words "frog" and "duck-ling" imitate the rhythmic value of quarter and eighth notes.

Activity 5: Mirror motions.

- As the recording of "Jazz Pizzicato" is playing, the children face you and follow as you lead movements that are short and quick.
- Begin seated using one hand, the other hand and both hands, then stand using one foot, the other foot, and then both feet.

Galump Went the Little Green Frog

Traditional

Ga - lump went the lit - tle green frog one day. Ga -

open fist   *close fist*   *open fist*
raise elbows   *lower elbows, etc.*
raise feet   *lower feet, etc.*

lump went the lit - tle green frog.   Ga - lump went the lit - tle green

close fist   *open fist*   *close fist*

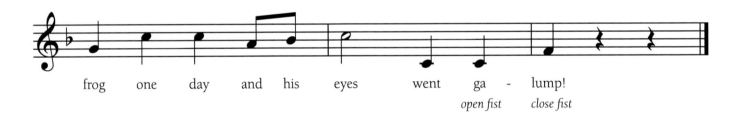

frog one day and his eyes went ga - lump!

                                            open fist   *close fist*

Activity 1: Sing "Galump Went the Little Green Frog."
- Sit on the floor. Sing "Galump Went the Little Green Frog" doing motions each time you sing the word "galump."
- I got the idea for these motions from Sophia Lopez Ibor when she taught a Spanish song about a frog. These are those motions: sing the song one time through using your fists—hold up both fists. When you sing "ga," open both fists, when you sing "lump," close both fists.
- Sing the song through again using different motions—raise your elbows (as in flapping wings) on "ga" and lower them on "lump."
- Sing the song again with these motions: raise your feet off the floor on "ga" and lower them on "lump." Sing the song again and do all three motions simultaneously.

Activity 2: Stand and do movements.
- Raise your foot on "ga" and stamp on "lump."
- It's fun to pause a bit each time you sing "ga" and hold the motion.

Good Day

Folk Song

When sheep get up in the morn - ing they al - ways say, "Good day!" —— When day!" "Baa, baa, baa, baa." That is what they say, they say. That is what they say.

Storybook: *Barn Dance*

Recording: "Corral Nocturne" and "Hoedown" from Aaron Copland's *Rodeo*

Activity 1: Introduce the song "Good Day."
- Sing and pat the steady beat on your knees.
- On the words of the animal voices, switch to clapping your hands, then back to patting your knees on the other words.
- Continue these actions as you sing for other farm animals.

Activity 2: Read the story *Barn Dance* as the recording of "Corral Nocturne" is playing in the background.
- When you are reading about the hoedown in the story, begin the recording of "Hoedown" (you probably will not have reached the end of the "Corral Nocturne" but that's ok).
- When you reach the end of the hoedown in the story, play the "Corral Nocturne" again and finish reading the story.

- Compare and contrast these two pieces of music. A nocturne is night music. The "Corral Nocturne" is quiet and gentle, perhaps a lullaby to put the animals to sleep. A hoedown is a lively dance.

Activity 3: Add percussion instruments.
- The children choose different percussion instruments to represent each animal's voice.
- Sing "Good Day" while patting the steady beat on your knees, as described in Activity 1, and play the appropriate percussion instrument when singing the words of the animal voices.

Activity 4: Ensemble.
- Review "Good Day" using the percussion instruments as described in Activity 3.
- Accompany the song with the following instruments: play percussion instruments when singing the words of the animal voices; play steady beat on C and G xylophone bars when singing the other words.

Hop Old Squirrel

Children's Song

Hop, old squirrel,   ei - dle dum, ei - dle dum. Hop, old squirrel,   ei - dle dum dee.

Hop, old squirrel,   ei - dle dum, ei - dle dum. Hop, old squirrel,   ei - dle dum dee.

Storybook: *The Busy Little Squirrel*
Recording: "Autumn" 2. Adagio Molto"
from Vivaldi's *The Four Seasons*

Activity 1: Introduce the song "Hop Old Squirrel."
- Teach the song while seated, using your hands to imitate the actions.
- Then, add the locomotor movement. Here are some ideas. The children can suggest other actions.

> Verse 1: Hop old squirrel...
> Verse 2: Jump old squirrel...
> Verse 3: Run old squirrel...
> Verse 4: Climb old squirrel...
> Verse 5: Swish your tail...
> Verse 6: Hunt for food...
> Verse 7: Sleep old squirrel...

Activity 2: Read the story *The Busy Little Squirrel* as the recording of "Autumn" is playing in the background.
- Teach musical vocabulary to describe this music: slow, gentle, peaceful.
- Ask what instruments are playing: string instruments.
- Contrast with *Flight of the Bumblebee* (see story "Buzz, Buzz, Busy Bees," p. 8).

Activity 3: Unstructured movement.
- As the recording of "Autumn" is playing, give each child a scarf. Suggest they pretend to be a leaf and move as though you are being blown by the wind.

Activity 4: Play a Sol-Mi game.
- For music educators, this game reinforces singing the intervals Sol to Mi.
- You will need lots of acorns. I collect them and keep them in my freezer until I'm ready to use them.

- Place the acorns on the floor around the sides of the room.
- Sit in a circle and pretend you are a nest of squirrels.
- Sing all the verses to "Hop Old Squirrel" and do the actions while seated.
- On the verse "hunt for food," tell the children they can go gather acorns but must come back to their places by the end of this verse. (Children should be familiar with the song and the length of each verse so they return to their place in time.)
- When back in the circle, each child counts his/her acorns and takes turns telling the class how many she or he gathered by singing, together with the class, that number.
- Sing the numbers on the pitches Sol and Mi (from G to E on resonator bells or xylophone) beginning with the number 1. For example, if a child collected 5 acorns, the class sings "1-2-3-4-5" on the pitches Sol, Mi, Sol, Mi, Sol (G-E-G-E-G). Use hand signs or body solfége to represent these two pitches.

Activity 5: Play a listening game.
- You will need one xylophone or other barred instrument.
- Set the xylophone in C pentatonic and place it in the center of the circle.
- Sing the song and play the game as described in Activity 4.
- After each child has collected acorns, instead of singing the number of acorns she or he has collected, each child comes to the xylophone and plays that number of times (on any bars).
- The class listens and silently counts the number of sounds they hear to determine how many acorns each classmate collected.
- You can use any percussion instrument for this activity if barred instruments are not available.

Let Us Chase the Squirrel

Traditional

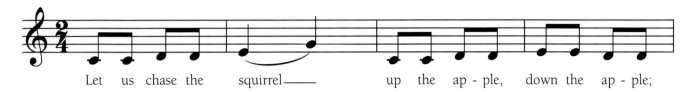

Let us chase the squirrel——— up the ap - ple, down the ap - ple;

Let us chase the squirrel——— up the ap - ple tree.

Activity 1: Sitting in a circle, sing "Let Us Chase the Squirrel" while patting the steady beat on your knees.
- Clap on the rest at the end of the song (after the word "tree").
- Transfer the clap to a triangle.
- Give children turns playing this part.

Activity 2: Play a game.
- Your first grade children can play this game. One child is "It," the roaming squirrel. The other children represent trees and squirrels and form groups of three: two children hold hands facing each other (trees), one stands in between them (squirrel). The roaming squirrel is alone and does not have a tree.
- Sing the song as the "trees" sway to the steady beat and the roaming squirrel walks about.
- At the end of the song, the "trees" raise their arms and let all the "squirrels" out to run and find a new tree.
- The "trees" keep their arms raised until they have a new "squirrel," then they lower their arms.
- There will be one child who did not find a tree. This child becomes the new roaming squirrel.
- To accompany the singing, some children can play the steady beat on C and G resonator bells or xylophone.

Activity 3: Focus on motion words.
- Focus on the words "up" and "down" when they occur in the song.
- Raise your arms up or down when you sing those words.
- Then, introduce the term "glissando."
- Hold a xylophone in a vertical position with the low bars parallel to the floor.
- Using one mallet, demonstrate a glissando up and a glissando down.
- Give children turns playing the glissando on the words "up" and "down."

Activity 4: Ensemble.
- Accompany the song "Let Us Chase the Squirrel" with the following instruments.
- Steady beat is played on C and G xylophone bars; rest played on triangle; glissandos played on xylophone on the words "up" and "down."

Hungry Caterpillar

Sally Guerrero

Hun - gry   lit - tle   ca - ter - pil - lar,   what's   for   lunch?

Storybook: *The Very Hungry Caterpillar*
Recording: "Morning Mood" from Edvard Grieg's *Peer Gynt Suite* No. 1, Op. 46

Activity 1: Introduce the chant "Hungry Caterpillar."
- Read the story *The Very Hungry Caterpillar* and sing the chant throughout the story.

Activity 2: Add resonator bells.
- Set up resonator bells (or xylophone) C, D, E, F, and G.
- Sing and play the melody.
- Teach the children to sing and play the ending G-G-C ("what's for lunch?").
- Children take turns playing this part on the bells.
- Some children will be able to play the entire melody if given the opportunity.

Activity 3: Add vegetables.
- Bring some fresh vegetables to class.
- Tell the "Hungry Caterpillar" story (without book) using these vegetables.
- It is fun to bring some unusual vegetables for the children to identify.
- Each time you bring out a new vegetable, sing the chant as a question.
- The children sing the answer on the pitches of Sol and Mi (from G to E on resonator bells or xylophone). For example, they would sing "car-rots" on the pitches of Sol and Mi, (G-E).

Activity 4: Begin the recording of "Morning Mood" to set the mood before reading the story.
- Begin reading the story *The Very Hungry Caterpillar* as the recording plays in the background.
- Teach musical vocabulary to describe this music: slow, gentle, peaceful, steady.
- Listen to the orchestra. You will hear a variety of instruments.

Activity 5: Play an unstructured movement game.
- Give the children one scarf, or two if you have enough.
- They pretend to be a caterpillar inside its cocoon and space themselves about the room on the floor with their scarf tucked underneath themselves.
- As the recording of "Morning Mood" plays, begin to tap one child at a time as a signal for them to come out of their cocoon and begin to fly.
- When all the children are "flying," play a stop and start game. The children freeze when you pause the music and move when you start the music again.

Activity 6: Mirror motions.
- Begin seated on the floor.
- Give each child one scarf, or two if you have enough, which they place on the floor in front of themselves.
- Play the recording of "Morning Mood" as you lead slow, sustained movements beginning with wiggling fingers on one hand, then the other, then both hands.
- Stand and pick up one scarf. Do arm movements.
- Pick up the second scarf and repeat movements with both arms.

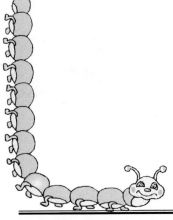

I Am a Fine Musician

German Folk Song
Adapted by Sally Guerrero

I am a fine mu-si-cian, I come from mu-sic land. I can play—

on my vi-o-lin. "Zum, zum, zum, zum, zum. Zum, zum, zum, zum, zum."

Storybook: *Mole Music*
Recording: "Spring" 3. Allegro from Vivaldi's *The Four Seasons*

Activity 1: Introduce "I Am A Fine Musician."
- The children pretend to play a violin as they sing.
- Sing about other instruments and pretend to play those.
- Create sounds to sing for each instrument such as "zum" for violin and "too" for trumpet. If you have pictures of these instruments, show them to the children.

Verse 1: ...I can play on my violin. Zum, zum, zum-zum, zum. Zum-zum, zum-zum, zum.

Verse 2: ...I can play on my trumpet. Too, too, too-too, toot. Too-too, too-too, toot.

Activity 2: Read the story *Mole Music* as the recording of "Spring" is playing in the background.
- Ask what instruments are playing: violins and other string instruments.

Activity 3: Extend Activity 2.
- Play the recording as you show the children the pictures from the book without reading the story out loud.
- Tell the children to remember the story and imagine what is happening as Mole practices his violin.

Activity 4: Do an art activity inspired by the messages in the story *Mole Music*.
- Discuss what these messages are: to play an instrument well, you must practice and not give up; music has the power to influence how we feel and can be a powerful force for good in the world.
- As "Spring" is playing in the background, the children draw something that the music inspires inside of them.
- Repeat the music several times until the children have completed their drawings.

I See the Moon

Traditional

I   see   the   moon   and   the   moon   sees   me.

We   are   as   hap - py   as   we   can   be.

Storybook: *Wynken, Blynken and Nod*
Recording: "Gnossiennes" No. 4 by Erik Satie

Activity 1: Introduce the song "I See the Moon."
- Pat the steady beat on your knees and add a clap on the rests (after "me" and after "be").
- Transfer the claps to a triangle.
- Give the children turns playing this part.

Activity 2: Read the story *Wynken, Blynken and Nod* as the recording of "Gnossiennes" is playing in the background.
- Teach musical vocabulary to describe this music: slow, smooth, floating, connected.
- Ask what instrument is playing: piano.

Activity 3: Act out a story about the night sky.
- The story will begin and end with the children mirroring you with free movement as a middle section.
- Everyone stands randomly about the space facing you.
- As the recording of "Gnossiennes" is playing, suggest the moon is rising as you raise your arms.
- Then, suggest the stars are coming out as you move one hand then the other slowly in front of you, wiggling your fingers.
- As a middle section, suggest that the children move quietly about the space and do a finger "dance" with other stars.
- Near the end of the music, quietly call the children to come back to mirror your movements as you place one hand, then the other, behind you as the stars go to rest.

Activity 4: Play a game on Sol-Mi.
- Music educators, here is a game to reinforce singing the pitches Sol to Mi (G to E on xylophone or resonator bells.)

- Draw faces on several paper plates; a happy, sad, angry, grumpy, sleepy face, etc. (For graphics, look for smiley face expressions on the Internet.)
- Prepare the children by identifying the emotions expressed on each face.
- Then, sing the song "I See the Moon" as you pat the beat and clap on the rests.
- At the end of the song, hold up one face.
- Sing a question on the pitches Sol and Mi: "Who sees a happy face?" (Sol Mi-Mi Sol-Sol Mi) (G E-E G-G E).
- Children echo sing, "We see a happy face," etc.
- Sing the song again, then hold up another face.
- Continue until you have sung for all your expressions.
- This can become a solo singing game.
- Hand out your paper plate faces to several children.
- Sing the song as an A section. Sing the question, "Who has the happy face?" as a B section.
- The child who has this plate responds by singing a solo, "I have the happy face."
- Repeat until you have sung about all the faces.

Activity 5: Ensemble and improvisation.
- Accompany the song "I See the Moon" with the following instruments. Steady beat is played on C and G xylophone bars (click mallets together on rests); triangles play on the rests.
- Sing the song as an A section using that accompaniment followed by an improvised B section.
- Set a metallophone or glockenspiel in C pentatonic.
- One child will improvise his or her idea for "moon music" on this instrument.
- Other children can play soft tremolos on triangles during the improvisation. I like to suggest the mood of moonlight and twinkling stars to set a soft and gentle mood for the improvised music.

I Went to Visit a Farm

Folk Song
Adapted by Sally Guerrero

I went to vis-it a farm one day. I heard a duck a-
I went to vis-it a farm one day. I heard a sound a-

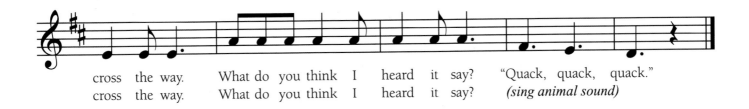

cross the way. What do you think I heard it say? "Quack, quack, quack."
cross the way. What do you think I heard it say? *(sing animal sound)*

Storybook: *Click, Clack Moo, Cows That Type*
Recording: "Fiddle Faddle" and "Typewriter"
    by Leroy Anderson

Activity 1: Introduce the song "I Went To Visit A Farm."
- Sing the song while patting the steady beat on your knees.
- When you sing the words for the animal voices, clap your hands.
- Ask the children to name some farm animals and sing about each animal.

Activity 2: Read the story *Click, Clack Moo, Cows That Type* as "Fiddle, Faddle" and "Typewriter" are playing in the background.
- Teach musical vocabulary to describe both of these pieces: fast, lively, energetic.
- Contrast with "Corral Nocturne" (see the story *Barn Dance*, p.15).

Activity 3: Play a game.
- You will need small plastic farm animals or small cut-out pictures of farm animals (see pp. 31–37).
- Hide one animal in your hand and sing the second version of "I Went To Visit A Farm" using the words "I heard a **sound** across the way." The children identify what animal you are hiding by the words you sing which imitates the animal's voice.

Activity 4: Encourage solo singing (when the children are familiar with the song).
- Distribute the farm animals to several children.
- Sing the first version of the song where you name the animal but stop singing just before the ending.
- The child who is holding the animal you have sung about sings a solo using the words that identify that animal's voice.

Ladybug

Sally Guerrero

La - dy bug, she creeps a - long. Here and there, ev - 'ry - where.

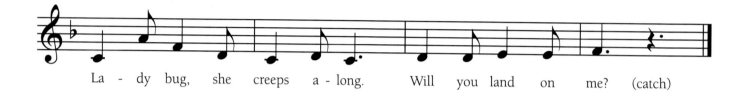

La - dy bug, she creeps a - long. Will you land on me? (catch)

Storybook: *Ten Little Ladybugs*
Recording: "Concerto Grosso in C Major,"
Op. 6 No. 10: V. Allegro by Corelli

Activity 1: Introduce the song "Ladybug."
- Sing while patting the steady beat on your knees and clapping on the last word, "catch."
- Give each child a pair of rhythm sticks.
- Sing the song while tapping the sticks to the steady beat.
- Ask each child to create a fancy way to play his/her sticks at the end of the song on the word "catch."
- Share each idea and have the class perform the ending using each child's idea.

Activity 2: Read the story *Ten Little Ladybugs* as the recording from *Concerto Grosso* is playing in the background.
- While reading to the beat of the music, I add the words, "How many ladybugs?" and count the ladybugs on each page before reading the text.
- Teach musical vocabulary to describe this music: fast, lively, energetic. Contrast with "Spring" (see the story *Mole Music,* p. 19).

Activity 3: Move to the beat.
- Play the recording from *Concerto Grosso* while doing steady beat motions.
- Invite children to take turns leading steady beat motions.

Activity 4: "Read" and clap the rhythm.
- For this activity, you will need ladybug cutouts which can be purchased from a school supply store (or you can draw your own).
- Tape 10 ladybugs to a poster board.
- The children clap their hands while counting for each ladybug as you point.
- Remove one ladybug.
- The children clap and count as you point.

Add the "rest."
- To teach the concept of "rest," draw the symbol for a quarter note rest on the back of each ladybug cutout.
- Instead of removing a ladybug, turn it over and tape it back in place to display the rest.
- The children clap one time for each ladybug and observe each rest.
- Later, you can transfer the claps to a percussion instrument.
- Both of these activities are good for eye/hand coordination, for reading and tracking from left to right, and for reinforcing the concept of "rest" in music.

Activity 5: Explore instruments.

- This game is nice for introducing and exploring xylophones or other percussion instruments.
- Set the xylophones in a pentatonic key.
- Follow the steps in Activity 4.
- As you point to the ladybugs, the children play any bars on their xylophone (or percussion instrument) and observe the rests.
- Children can take turns pointing as their classmates play.

Activity 6: Play a passing game.

- You will need a "ladybug" which you can make. I purchased two large red pom-poms at an art supply store, glued them together, and wrapped a black pipe cleaner around them for wings.
- All sit in a circle.
- Choose one child to be "It" and sit in the center of the circle with eyes closed.
- Sing the song "Ladybug" and begin passing the ladybug to the right.
- On the word "catch," the child holding the ladybug, including everyone else, hides their hands.
- The child who is "It" gets three chances to guess who has the ladybug.
- A new child is chosen to be "It" and the game continues.

Activity 7: Extend the game.

- With older children, play the passing game as described in Activity 6, but add this new twist: sing "Ladybug" and begin passing the ladybug to the right.
- On the words "here," "there," "every," "where," add this variation: the child who has the ladybug on the word "here" passes it back on the word "there" to the child who just had it.
- These two children pass it back and forth again to the words "every" and "where" and then resume passing it in the original direction.
- On the word "catch," the child holding the ladybug, including everyone else, hides their hands.
- "It" guesses who has the ladybug.

Pitter, Patter

Pit - ter, pat - ter, pit - ter, pat - ter, lis - ten to the rain.

Pit - ter, pat - ter, pit - ter, pat - ter, on my win - dow pane.

Storybook: *Yellow Umbrella*

Recording: "Petite Ouverture à Danser" by Erik Satie

Activity 1: Introduce the song "Pitter, Patter."
- Sing the song and pat the steady beat in different places (head, shoulders, etc.).

Activity 2: Present the story *Yellow Umbrella* as the recording of "Petite Ouverture A Danser" is playing in the background. (This book comes with a CD, however I prefer to use the recording of "Petite Ouverture à Danser.")
- Ask the children if the music is describing a storm or a gentle rain: gentle rain.
- Teach music vocabulary to describe this music: slow, gentle, peaceful.
- Ask what instrument is playing: piano.
- Contrast with "The Happy Farmer" (see the story *Barnyard Dance*, p.5).

Activity 3: Do a movement activity.
- This is a semi-structured movement activity: you will need a colored scarf for each child and colored construction paper to match each scarf color.
- Begin seated.
- Play the recording "Petite Ouverture à Danser" for this activity.
- The children move with their scarves when you display the color of paper that matches their scarf and sit when you take it away. You can display several colors at a time.

- Encourage the children to move with slow, sustained movements.
- This is good practice for their impulse control and for building visual skills.
- Students must also dance carefully around those children who are seated.

Activity 4: Do a movement and listening activity.
- This movement activity reinforces very focused listening skills and is suited for older children.
- Choose three or four sets of colored scarves and distribute one to each child.
- Assign each color a number.
- For example, yellow is number 1, blue is number 2, and red is number 3.
- When you tap a finger cymbal 1, 2, or 3 times, the children with the color that corresponds to that number may move.
- When you play that number again, they sit still until you play their number again.
- Use the recording "Petite Ouverture à Danser" during this activity.

Activity 5: Ensemble.
- Accompany the song "Pitter, Patter" with these instruments: steady beat is played on D and A xylophone bars; add clusters of tones played randomly on a glockenspiel (set in D pentatonic). Other random "rain" sounds can be played on triangles, sticks, etc.

Squiggle

Theme: Maurice Ravel, *Empress of the Pagodas*
Lyrics: Sally Guerrero

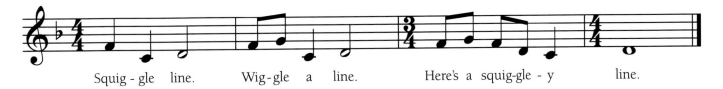

Squig - gle line. Wig - gle a line. Here's a squig-gle - y line.

Storybook: *The Squiggle*
Recording: "Empress of the Pagodas" from Maurice Ravel's *Mother Goose Suite III*

Activity 1: Read the story *The Squiggle* as the recording of "Empress of the Pagodas" is playing in the background.

- Describe the many contrasts found in this music: sometimes smooth and slow, sometimes bouncy and fast; listen for the gong.
- Contrast with "Morning Mood" (see the story *The Very Hungry Caterpillar*, p. 18).
- When you have finished reading the story, ask the children to recall the different squiggle shapes and ask which was their favorite.
- Tell the children you can "sing" the squiggle shapes.
- Look at various shapes throughout the book and vocalize on a neutral syllable as you point with your finger and follow the contour of the line with your singing voice. For example, if the contour of the line begins low and goes up, start singing on a low tone and slide up to a high tone.

Activity 2: Introduce the song "Squiggle." (Notice this melody is taken from the middle section of "Empress of the Pagodas.")

- Sing the song several times as the children listen. Then, ask them to join you in singing together.
- If this is a good time, ask the children to listen to the recording again and join in singing when they hear this melody in the recording. Also ask them to focus on the use of the gong in the music.
- Using a red marker, draw a different squiggle shape on your white board.
- Vocalize together as you follow the contour of the line with your finger and the children follow singing on a neutral syllable. I like the children to also use their finger to "draw" the shape in the air as they are vocalizing.
- Alternate singing the song with children coming to the board to draw their own squiggle shapes for the class to "sing."

Activity 3: Purchase a ball of thick, red yarn at a craft store. Use 30 or 40 feet (or more) of this to create a large circular, wavy or jagged path on the floor of your classroom.

- Play the recording "Empress of the Pagodas" while inviting 1 or 2 children at a time to follow the path by walking/jumping/skipping from one end of it to the other.
- Ask them to match their movements to the movement of the music.
- Give the children opportunities to design another path.

Activity 4: This game is for older children.

- Give each child a red marker and a sheet of paper.
- Each child designs his/her own squiggle shape. Collect them and choose four sheets to place on the board where the class can see.
- Select one child who will secretly decide on one of the four squiggles.
- As the class watches, this child walks a path around the room that matches the contour of the chosen design.
- The class guesses which of the four designs the child walked.
- Whoever guesses correctly goes next.

Activity 5: Ensemble and improvisation: music educators, you can use the image of the squiggle line as a metaphor for a musical line.

- Explain that sometimes a melody is called a melodic line. It can go from high to low, weave around, leap, etc.
- Set your barred instruments in the key of F pentatonic. Metallophones sound very nice with this.
- As an A section, the children accompany the singing of "Squiggle" with a steady beat played on D and A.
- Children take turns improvising a B section on a xylophone. Here is where they will design their melodic line and be as creative as they like.
- As each child takes a solo turn to play his/her B section, the class can softly tremolo on long bar D.
- Other children can add the sound of a gong or finger cymbals to create texture and color.

Three Little Snowmen

Melody: Sally Guerrero
Lyrics: Traditional*

Three lit-tle snow-men fat. Each with a fun-ny hat. Out came the sun and mel-ted one. Now, what do you think of that? Down, down, down.

Storybook: *The Snowman*
Recording: "Theme from the Snowman"
Recording: "Walking In the Air"

Activity 1: Introduce the song "Three Little Snowmen."
- Sing while patting the steady beat on your knees.
- Add a clap on the rests after the words "fat," "hat," and "that."
- Show a descending motion on the words "down, down, down."

Activity 2: Read the story *The Snowman* as the recording of "Theme from the Snowman" is playing in the background. Following is a very enchanting activity I do at the end of the story:
- I made a large, white, scarf parachute with material I purchased in the bridal section of a fabric store. It is about 120 inches in width and I cut it into a large circle. As the music "Theme from the Snowman" plays, I bring this out.
- The children gather around and hold it as they would a parachute and slowly raise and lower it to the music.
- I give the children paper snowflakes (which they made) to toss onto the parachute.

- As we continue to raise and lower it, the snowflakes flutter about.
- Near the end of the music, we set the parachute on the floor.
- I ask the children to close their eyes and I place a stuffed snowman in the center of the circle.
- When they open their eyes, they are amazed to find that another snowman has magically appeared.

Activity 3: Play another recording from the video *The Snowman* called "Walking In the Air," which is sung by a boy soprano. For the boys in your class, it is a wonderful example of a boy's singing voice.
- You can repeat the parachute activity as described in Activity 2 while this music is playing.

Activity 4: Sing "Three Little Snowman" as in Activity 1.
- Transfer the claps to finger cymbals.
- Play G-E-C on resonator bells or glockenspiel when singing the words "down, down, down."

Activity 5: Ensemble.
- Accompany the song "Three Little Snowmen" with the following instruments: steady beat is played on C and G xylophone bars; finger cymbals play on rests; glockenspiel plays G-E-C on "down, down, down."

*From *Kodàly in Kindergarten* by Katinka S. Daniel.

What Shall We Do When We All Go Out?

Traditional

What shall we do when we all go out, all go out, all go out?

What shall we do when we all go out, when we all go out to play?

Storybook: *The Snowy Day*

Recording: "Morning Has Broken" with Brian Dunning & Jeff Johnson

Recording: "Skater's Waltz" by Émile Waldteufel

Activity 1: Introduce the song "What Shall We Do When We All Go Out?"

- To prepare for the story, ask children what they can do outside on a snowy day. (If you don't live where it snows, create a discussion around what it is like to live in a cold climate.)
- Each time you sing the song, one child pantomimes an activity.
- The class guesses what it is.

Activity 2: Unstructured movement.

- Suggest that the children move like a snowflake as you play a triangle (play soft tremolos).
- When you stop playing, the children freeze into an interesting shape.
- When you begin playing again, the children begin moving.
- Notice different shapes and poses you see and make comments such as "I see tall snowflakes," "I see small snowflakes," "I see round snowflakes," "I see flat snowflakes."
- Continue with comments that encourage the children to explore different shapes.

Activity 3: Read the story *The Snowy Day* as the recording of "Morning Has Broken" is playing in the background.

Activity 4: Act it out.

- Lynn Kleiner describes this activity in her book *Kids Can Listen, Kids Can Move*.
- After reading the story, recall the sequence of what Peter did when he went out to play.
- Play the recording of "Morning Has Broken" as the class pantomimes Peter's actions.

Activity 5: Imaginative play.

- At the end of the story, Peter and his friend go outside to have more adventures.
- Suggest that they might go ice-skating.
- Tell the children you can pretend to ice skate in the classroom.
- Distribute two paper plates to each child (use thin plates).
- Play the recording of "Skater's Waltz."
- The children put the skates under their shoes and "skate" about the room.
- Play "stop and start."
- Pause the music and tell the children to freeze until the music begins again.

Who's Hatching From the Egg?

Sally Guerrero

I - won - der who____ is hatch - ing from the egg?____ I

won - der who____ is hatch - ing from the egg?

Solo or echo

It's a ba - by di - no - saur.   Hel - lo, ba - by di - no - saur.

Story Book: *Who's Hatching?*

Recording: "Ballet of the Unhatched Chicks" from Mussorgsky's *Pictures At An Exhibition*

Activity 1: Read the story.

- Read the sliding board book story *Who's Hatching?* as the recording "Ballet of the Unhatched Chicks" is playing in the background. As you read, jiggle each sliding page a bit before opening the page fully.

- Tell the children to "rumble" their hands on their knees as you jiggle each page. By "rumble," I mean to alternate patting their knees quickly. When you open the page fully, this is the signal for the children to stop "rumbling." This activity is good for eye/hand coordination. Continue in a similar manner for each page.

- I usually read half the book in one lesson and the other half in another lesson. If you read the entire book, you will need to replay the recording one time.

Activity 2: Dance to the recording of "Ballet of the Unhatched Chicks."

- Children pretend to be an unhatched chick, or another animal they choose, in its egg. They pantomime the animal pecking or scratching, etc. to get out.

- Once each "animal" has hatched, the children can make up their own dance to imitate their animal. Classroom teachers, this is a good activity and story to correlate with a science project!

Activity 3: Play another game using the recording.

- Children secretly decide what animal they will be. Of course, it has to be an animal that hatches.

- Choose one child to pantomime his or her dance which replicates the animal she or he has chosen.

- The class guesses what animal it might be. Whoever guesses correctly gets to go next!

Activity 4: Make a craft project.

- For this activity, you will need several large plastic eggs which you can purchase at a craft store. You will also need some small plastic animals that hatch from eggs such as a spider, bird, caterpillar, or tadpole to put inside each egg. I made a spider with a black pipe cleaner, a caterpillar with a green pipe cleaner, and a tadpole with a black pipe cleaner. You can also find plastic animals at a school supply store such as fish, dinosaurs, etc.

- Introduce the chant "Who's Hatching From the Egg?" as an echo.

- Bring out one of the eggs as you are singing the chant.

- After singing the first part of the chant, shake the egg as the children "rumble" their hands on their knees until you stop. Vary the length of time you shake the egg each time.

- Allow the children to guess what animal might be inside the egg, then open it and sing the second part of the song. This is a good activity for eye/hand coordination.

Activity 5: Play a rhythm game using the colored eggs.

- You will need four blue eggs (or pink) and four yellow eggs.
- The words "blue" and "yel-low" will become spoken patterns using the rhythm of the language. Music educators will understand that this language imitates the rhythmic value of quarter and eighth notes.
- Place a combination of four eggs on the floor in front of you where the children can see.
- Recite the pattern so that the children are tracking from their left to right as they observe the pattern. A pattern could read "yel-low, blue, yel-low, blue" and so forth.
- Let the children create and read patterns using different color combinations of four eggs.

Activity 6: Do a steady beat activity using shaker eggs.

- You can make your own shaker eggs using plastic Easter eggs and fill them with about a tablespoon full of rice. Seal each egg using a hot glue gun.
- Give each child two eggs.
- As the music "Ballet of the Unhatched Chicks" is playing, create ideas for keeping the steady beat using the two eggs. The children can follow your ideas and they can create their own new steady beat ideas for the class to follow.

Activity 7: Extending the activity with instruments.

- Music educators, this activity serves several purposes: as a good introduction to xylophones and as an opportunity for solo singing and leadership. It also establishes eye/hand coordination and the skill of following the conductor.
- Set your xylophones (or other barred instruments) in C pentatonic.
- One child is chosen to be the conductor/leader.
- The conductor holds a shaker egg and conducts the steady beat as the class accompanies their singing by playing a steady beat on the bars C and G.
- After singing the first part of the song, the conductor shakes the egg as the class "rumbles" on any bars they like. They must stop "rumbling" when the conductor stops.
- Allow the conductor several chances to lead this part as the class follows.
- Finally, the conductor sings a solo to identify what animal she or he imagines is hatching from the egg.

I See A Song
Art Project

Recordings: **Your choice**

Activity 1: Present the story, *I See A Song* while one of the recordings you have collected from those suggested in this book is playing in the background.
- When you have finished, ask the children which was their favorite picture in the book.

Activity 2: Do an art project.
- This is an art project that offers more opportunities for the children to hear the recordings suggested in this book.
- Tell the children they will be creating their own *I See A Song* book.

- You will need one sturdy, white sheet of paper for each child and pieces of colored construction paper, cut into small pieces, for the children to use to create their picture.
- The children design their picture by gluing pieces of construction paper onto the white paper.
- When each child has completed his or her picture, put them all together in a folder or binder.
- Let the children see their completed book.
- Then let them choose which recording they would like to go with their book. You can give them several choices using the recordings suggested in this book.
- When they have made their decision, present their book to them with the recording they have chosen.

Reproducible Activity Art

Bibliography & Discography

Here are some tips for using the following resources; some of the books you will already have in your school library, and some you can purchase "used" on Amazon.com.

If you go to the iTunes Store to purchase the music, on the home page, click on *power search*. When that page comes up, under *all results*, click on *music*. This gives you additional options for typing in composer, album and genre which are very helpful in finding exactly what you will need. Be aware that if an album goes out of print, the album I have specified may not be found. In that case, leave out the particular album in order to find the music.

Storybook: *Barn Dance* by Bill Martin, Jr. and John Archambault, ISBN 0-8050-0799-7.

Recording: In iTunes under composer, type in: Aaron Copland; under song, type in: Corral Nocturne, then type in: Hoedown.

Storybook: *Barnyard Dance*, board book by Sandra Boynton, ISBN 13: 978-1-56305-442-6.

Recording: In iTunes under song, type in: The Happy Farmer; under composer, type in: Schumann; under artist, type in: Evelyne Dubourg.

Storybook: *Busy Little Squirrel, The* by Nancy Tafuri, ISBN 0-68987341-7.

Recording: In iTunes under song, type in: The Four Seasons Concerto in F Major; under composer, type in: Vivaldi; (when the music comes up, look for "Autumn" II. Adagio Molto).

Storybook: *Buzz, Buzz, Busy Bees* by Dawn Bentley, ISBN 0-689-86848-0.

Recording: In iTunes under song, type in: Flight of the Bumblebee; under composer, type in: Rimsky-Korsakov; under album, type in: The Most Popular Classical TV Themes in the Universe (I chose this album for its slightly slower tempo.)

Storybook: *Click, Clack, Moo Cows That Type* by Doreen Cronin, ISBN 0-689-83213-3.

Recording: In iTunes under song, type in: Fiddle Faddle (then type in Typewriter); under composer, type in: Leroy Anderson; under artist, type in: Richard Hayman (I chose this artist for the slightly slower tempo.)

Storybook: *I See A Song* by Eric Carle, ISBN 0-590-25213-5.

Recordings: Any of the recordings recommended in this book.

Storybook: *Jump, Frog, Jump* by Robert Kalan, ISBN 0-688-09241-1.

Recording: In iTunes under song, type in: Jazz Pizzicato; under composer, type in: Leroy Anderson; under artist, type in: Richard Hayman.

Storybook: *Little Cloud* by Eric Carle, ISBN 0-698-11830-8.

Recording: In iTunes under song, type in: No. 2 from Four Norwegian Dances, Op. 35; under composer, type in: Edvard Grieg.

Storybook: *Mole Music* by David McPhail, ISBN 0-8050-2819-6.

Recording: In iTunes under song, type in: The Four Seasons Concerto in E Major; under composer, type in: Vivaldi; (when the music comes up, look for "Spring" III. Allegro.)

Storybook: *Snowman, The* by Raymond Briggs, (Step Into Reading) available through www.randomhouse.com/kids. Go to this website and type in: The Snowman; look for the "Early Step Into Reading" book. The ISBN number is 0-679-89443-8.

Recording: In iTunes under song, type in: Theme From the Snowman; under artist, type in: Sang Froid; under album, type in: The Christmas Chillout Collection; under genre, type in: Holiday.

Recording: In iTunes under song, type in: Walking In the Air; under artist, type in: Peter Auty; under genre, type in: Children's Music.

Storybook: *Snowy Day, The* by Jack Keats, ISBN 0-14-050182-7.

Recording: In iTunes under song, type in: Morning Has Broken; under artist, type in: Brian Dunning; under album, type in: Stars in the Morning East - A Christmas Meditation; under genre, type in: Holiday. (This is an instrumental version of the song which you need in order to read the story as the music is playing.)

Recording: In iTunes under song, type in: Skater's Waltz; under composer, type in: Waldteufel; under album, type in: The Very Best Christmas Selections.

Storybook: *Squiggle, The* by Carole Lexa Schaefer, ISBN 0-517-88579-4.

Recording: In iTunes under song, type in Empress of the Pagodas; under composer, type in Ravel; under artist, type in Charles Munch.

Storybook: *Ten Little Ladybugs* by Melanie Gerth, ISBN 158117091-2.

Recording: In iTunes under song, type in: Concerto Grosso in C Major, Op. 6 No. 10: V. Allegro; under composer, type in: Corelli; under artist, type in: Roy Goodman.

Storybook: *Ugly Duckling, The* retold by Harriet Ziefert, illustrated by Emily Bolam, ISBN: 0-14-038352-2

Recording: In iTunes under song, type in: The Swan; under composer, type in: Saint Saens; under album, type in: The Essential Yo Yo Ma.

Storybook: *Very Hungry Caterpillar, The* by Eric Carle, ISBN 0-590-03029-9.

Recording: In iTunes under song, type in: Morning Mood; under composer, type in: Edvard Grieg; under album, type in: The Ultimate Children's Classical Collection.

Storybook: *Very Lonely Firefly, The* by Eric Carle, ISBN 0-399-23427-6.

Recording: In iTunes under song, type in: Forgotten Dreams; under composer, type in: Leroy Anderson; under album, type in: Stars and Stripes, An American concert.

Storybook: *Who's Hatching? A Sliding Surprise Book* by Charles Reasoner, ISBN 0-8431-0598-4.

Recording: In iTunes under song, type in: Ballet of the Unhatched Chicks; under composer, type: Modest Mussorgsky; under artist, type: Bournemouth.

Storybook: *Wynken, Blynken and Nod* illustrated by Johanna Westerman, ISBN 1-55858-422-6. (I prefer the book illustrated by Susan Jeffers. It is out of print but available as a used book on some websites), ISBN 0-14-054794-0.

Recording: In iTunes under song, type in: Gnossiennes No. 4; under composer, type in: Erik Satie; under artist, type in: Pascal Roge; under album, type in: 3 Gymnopedies.

Storybook: *Yellow Umbrella* illustrated by Jae Soo Liu, ISBN 1-929132-36-0.

Recording: In iTunes under song, type in: Petite Ouverture a Danser; under composer, type in: Erik Satie; under artist, type in: Reinbert de Leeuw (I prefer this artist because of the tempo.)